Down the alley of Surprises!

by Shamik Dhar

ACKNOWLEDGEMENT

I am thankful to my parents, family members and friends for their support without which this book would not have seen the light of day. I am grateful to Mr. Prabir Sen my brother-in-law and Dr. Madhabendhu Dhar, my uncle who has helped me with the illustrations.

ABOUT THE BOOK:

I started writing this book when I was nineteen. I have given my heart and soul to nurture this book. Possibly after twenty-three years now, I have managed to see the funny side of life. Having studied in India, U.K and the U.S., I have composed my stories in an Indian backdrop. I tried to add an international flavour of the funny side of composing the stories. Some of the stories are actual real life stories. In the times of COVID, when everyone is stressed out. I have tried to put back that refreshing smile on everyone's faces. That is the motive of the book.

Table of Contents

IT'S ALL ON THE CARDS!

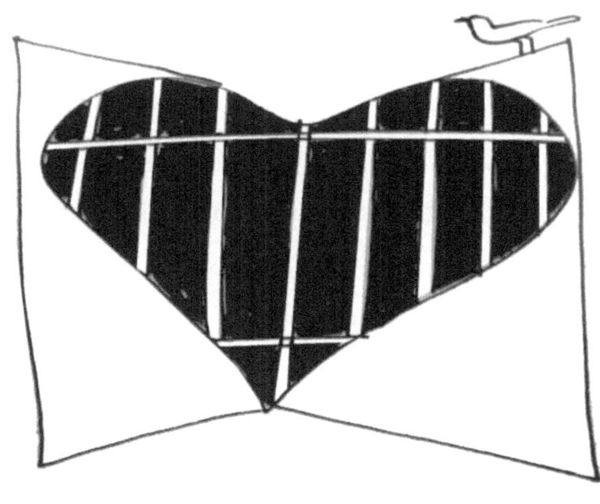

T he other day, Suman had said, "You never send me any cards, be it Christmas, New Year's Eve, or Diwali."

He was one of those guys who was meticulous in maintaining these courtesies. I didn't have any appropriate answer. Frankly speaking, I am pretty helpless on this issue. It's not that I forget, nor is it the lack of interest to keep the fragile flame of friendship burning, but somehow it always turns out that way.

To tell you the truth, I find it practically impossible to select a card for a specific personality. Whenever you send a card to someone it should always have your personal touch, be in accordance with the tastes of that personality you are sending to, and associated with an acute aesthetic touch. According to some, the contents of the card do not matter. They say, "It's always the love that is associated with it." I beg to differ on this issue because, it is always the contents of the cards that matters. That is probably why so many card shops have sprouted up.

I am completely lost whenever I enter a card shop. The sheer bulk of the cards arranged neatly in the racks tend to confuse me. Even though, there are various sections on the racks that classify the cards. They tend to highlight the colour of the changing festive occasions and the changing seasons of the heart but also in accordance to the myriad confusion of relations. However, the predominant section is conferred upon the young love and cupid. Thus, it is the pleas of the enmeshed emotions, which reigned supreme.

Being young and romantic, I too, in fact, was not spared from Cupid's antics. The eyes had mesmerized and captivated me. I had the feeling that I could immerse myself in the depths of those eyes. Whenever I met her, I wished I could let my heart speak, yet somehow it was quite impossible. The rational intellect insisted that there would always be a next time. The next time was probably tomorrow and that tomorrow never arrived. My intellect became the slave of my heart. It forced me to express my throbbing emotions somehow. It was then that I decided to visit my nearest card shop in search for some appropriate remedy.

As I pushed open the door, the owner greeted me with a smile and his enormous tiger moustache. I smiled back innocently at the man whose moustache were curled, enough to balance a crow at each end. Quite confidently, I started the work. It didn't take me long to submerge myself into the maze of relations. It was after almost half an hour later, I realized that I was completely lost.

When I looked up, I saw that Sourav, my pal, was also approaching the card shop. I could clearly see him through the tinted glass walls of the exquisitely decorated card shop. Well, if he somehow came to know of my weakness, then the whole world would too. It was a panic, selecting a card before Valentine's Day, well nothing short of Hara-Kiri!

I randomly selected a card from the special friend's section. I chose one that was simple and had a hell of a lot of daffodils. Out of sheer panic, I handed the card to the shopkeeper who quickly took note of its price, which he scribbled down on a notepad.

Just as he was about to hand me the card, I stopped him. "Just a minute!" I said.

The cascading flow of his handwriting caught my attention. I quickly asked him to write a message to express how I truly felt , to capture my emotions, the thoughts that had been raging inside me for so long. I decided to keep it short and simple. While the shopkeeper was writing it down, I was watching Sourav. He didn't seem his usual bubbly self as if lost somewhere. It was evident by the way he made his way, trying to elude the ever-increasing vehicular congestion that blocked his progress. The shopkeeper quickly wrote down my heart's message, put the card back inside the envelope, and placed it on the desk. Sourav was about to open the tinted glass door when I placed the card and slid behind one of the racks so that he would miss me. He had missed me. He was heading straight for the valentine's section, which surprised me even more.

I pulled myself out from behind the rack, pocketed the change, and quickly slid the precious envelope under my shirt. Now, it was my turn to catch him red handed. I realized that he too was in the process of sending out a heart racking message to his would-be sweetheart. Strangely, he managed to select a card in no time, which annoyed me. As he was heading for the payment counter, I crept behind him and tapped his shoulder. Poor guy, he was almost shocked out of his senses when he turned. Well, I was the last person on earth he was expecting. I twitched both my eyebrows and gave him one of those looks that said, "Got you, man!"

There could be no excuse because the previous day we two had spoken at length in order to convince the other mutual friends of the futility of sending such messages that could be better dealt with by speaking face to face with the beloved. Well, he turned red and started shaking all over. I decided to give him a break and said, "Well, well!"

I continued, "I will promise to keep this under wraps for the time being if you want, but only if you reveal the identity of the person whom you are sending that card!" He meekly nodded and blurted out the name of the lady and scampered out just like a rabbit after paying the price of sharing such a secret of his with me.

Thanking God, I too ran out. I did not follow him but decided to carry off this mission of mine secretly. He too, must have been thanking his stars for getting rid of me so easily for the time being. It was late, so I went straight for the post office and posted my fate with a five-rupee stamp. Waiting for the deliverance scared me. I was in a worse position than Sourav because he could now speak of his fears and aspirations to me. I on the other hand couldn't as I was afraid to let go of my dominant position as an individual who is unaffected by such trifle emotions as "Love." Whenever the phone rang, I assumed it to be from the queen of my heart. The restless feeling continued to haunt me. It tore me limb by limb yet there was no way out.

One fine afternoon, the phone rang. Only after I had picked it up, did I realize it was from none other than my beloved.

"Did you send me a card, Shamik?"

I meekly admitted in the affirmative.

She asked, "Can you come to the District Park now?"

"Now?"

She said, "Yes!"

"Why not? I will make it!" I said.

Then the line went dead. There were butterflies in my stomach. Well, hope springs eternal. I had to make it. My heart seemed willing to pop out of my mouth. I couldn't stop myself from trying to out jump my leaping heart and stopped only when I realized my younger brother was watching me wide-eyed. I quickly shaved and drenched myself in denim before rushing to her. It was dusk and although the moon was strangely lost somewhere, she stood like Diana, the moon goddess. I tried to get her so close that I could touch her. My rational mind forbids me from doing so.

It was then she delivered her response. "Take your card and go to hell!" she spat as the ashes of my hopes lay scattered.

With due regards to my "crush" and the special friend's section, I must admit it was the last time I ever sent a card to anyone. When I opened the envelope, out fell the daffodils. The testimony of my misfortune, and it was perchance that I happened to open it to have a last look. Even though the message bore her name on top, and it was printed in plain simple English, "Happy Birthday." The three-letter word that followed this "Happy Birthday" was quite a misfit. It was "Mom." Underneath, this three letter word was scripted my proud name "Shamik Dhar." Being the joker, let me dedicate this to the queen of my heart!

****

CAT AND MICE

She had walked in and asked, "Can I have a seat Didi?" Then she had introduced herself saying, "I am Anima. I work with the police."

She said, "What a slip of the tongue!"

She then went on to say, "Thank God, I found you all. I was afraid to travel all alone in a single train compartment!"

Who needed whose company was really not evident. We had to be assured that the police were there for the protection of the commoners, with the induction of Anima in the second compartment of the train.

Anima continued, "Have you ever been to the Sagar mela?"

Though we had been traveling to the Sagar islands once in a while, we had never visited it during the mela time. There were far too many people for us to be comfortable.

Indranil replied, "Unfortunately, Yes!"

"Ok! You know my idol is Kiran Bedi!" she had continued.

Kiran Bedi is the pride of Indian Police Force. She is modern, media savvy and dedicated. Hence, it was natural.

Indranil enquired, "How long did you say you are working in the force?"

She grinned and replied, "Three years!"

Wiping the end of her mouth with the tip of her saree she added, "Inspector Chowdhury, says if I work well the next two years I might be promoted!"

Mr. Bhattacharyya was trying to appear bored but I could feel he was on his toes. He stretched his body and then lit a cigarette to soothe his nerves.

Anima the constable said, "Didi, where are you all going?"

Indranil appeared stressed as he made that crackling noise by cracking his fingers. He was a bit nervous, I felt.

I replied, "Kolkata…And you?" trying to divert her attention.

"Bonga"

"Are you not afraid to work as a constable?"

She smiled and replied, "No, No I am no longer afraid! The

inspector says one should fight fear. The only fear that I have is him!"

Anima continued, "I was afraid of thieves when I first started, but then I was put on duty as plainclothes police woman. So most people didn't know I was in the police! "

Indranil whose one profession was looking after the export business that he inherited from his father asked, "Why? Are you afraid of your own inspector?"

Before she could reply, the train came to a jolting stop. Mr. Bhattacharyya looked at Indranil and said, "Indra, take a look!"

Indranil reluctantly left his seat and his big shoulder bag and went to have a look. I wiped the sweat from my forehead with the end of my saree and clutched my leather handbag closer to my breast. We were not accustomed to returning home with so much cash. It made all three of us nervous and jittery. Mr. Bhattacharyya was slowly getting impatient. He pressed the butt of his cigarette on the ashtray attached to the wall of the train between the two windows. He stood up and once again stretched.

Indranil who was by now stretching his neck out of the open door said, "No signal, I had guessed correctly!"

He turned towards Mr. Bhattacharyya, raised his eyebrows and gave him a questioning look.

Mr. Bhattacharyya said, "Indra, relax there is no need to jump out of the train!"

Everyone laughed at this. Indranil returned and tried to make himself comfortable once again on the seat. The seat consisted of nothing but of a couple of wooden planks held together with an iron frame. By then Mr. Bhattacharyya, had already taken a seat.

Anima continued, "Do you know there was a robbery on this train four or five days ago?"

I looked at Mr. Bhattacharyya and then at Anima and replied, "Really!"

She said, "Relax there is no chance of having one today."

The comment appeared to be humorous to her, as she was in splits. I could feel the heat and humidity getting to me. The ceiling fans were churning out a lot of noise but they were hardly providing any respite from the intolerable heat.

Mr. Bhattacharyya said, "Anima, you didn't say why you were afraid of your inspector?"

By now, Anima had taken a big aluminium can out of her jute handbag and was taking out some pieces of coconut kernel. She gave one to Indranil and one to Mr. Bhattacharyya. He refused politely and so did I.

She insisted for some time and then replied, "Do you really want to know?"

I said, "Why not?"

Indranil however intervened and asked, "What is the time now?"

Mr. Bhattacharyya looked at his wristwatch and replied, "It's half-past six."

As I turned towards Anima, I could see the last remnants of the dying sunrays. The black shroud of darkness was rapidly enveloping the green countryside.

Anima munched on one white coconut kernel piece and mumbled, "I joined the force when I was twenty-one."

She continued, "I was assigned as a plain clothes policewoman at the Ganga Sagar Mela."

Indranil injected, "We are also returning from the Sagar islands."

Anima exclaimed, "Really!"

Suddenly the train jolted up and started moving. The squeaking of the wheels was a relief to us.

Mr. Bhattacharyya asked casually, "Anima, how many thieves have you caught?"

She started counting with her right-hand thumb stopping at the ends of the fingers. Then she replied, "Maybe six or seven. Why? Are you thieves?"

I said, "You must be very brave then!" trying to divert the matter.

"I am just an ordinary policewoman, working undercover. Why? Are you thieves?"

Indranil said, "Why? Do we look like thieves?"

She turned towards me and replied, "Not really." and then smiled.

By then we had reached the next station. We could not see the name of the station since it was pitch dark and there was no electricity at the station. All we could see was a hawker selling a mixture of puffed rice and chanachor. An oil lamp shone timidly and its radiance was no good for comfort. A big guy now boarded the train. He smelled of hooch and appeared to be totally drunk. He ambled across and stopped beside our seat. He looked at Indranil and then at Anima. He mumbled something incomprehensible to Anima and turned his attention towards Indranil. The drunk saluted him and showed his ticket and settled in one of the adjacent seat little ahead of us. Indranil in his black coat and white trousers must have appeared to be a ticket collector to him. When we realized it, we laughed. The train started moving and slowly gathered pace.

Anima now became a little quieter and she almost whispered, "Inspector Rakhal Chowdhury is my boss. He is an honest man. I have never ever seen him take a bribe. He is the best."

Then she lowered her voice and said, "The only time I saw him embarrassed was when the famous pickpocket Jhanu was about to be caught in front of the public shouted out "Hello brother! Are you taking me home? Didn't I send you your paycheck?'"

I couldn't help laughing even in the tension. Mr. Bhattacharyya even smiled.

Indranil was as his own fidgety self. He asked, "Is it true?"

Anima replied, "Depends on what you believe in!"

"It is very difficult task to make thieves speak sometimes. They never say where they hide their stolen loot." she said.

She turned towards Mr. Bhattacharyya and answered, "Sometimes you have to torture them to make them speak."

I asked, "Do you do that too?"

She tilted her head and replied, "No. Usually the men do it. Sometimes they are hung upside down and wrapped in a blanket and beaten with sticks till they admit they have committed the crime!"

She said, "There are other ways to make them speak too!"

She continued, "The worst part of it is that whenever we want some action, the political interventions stop us from doing it. Some of them get out on bail and we feel we should shoot them. Inspector Chowdhury says he will shoot every bastard down if he had a chance!"

Indranil asked, "Is that why you are afraid of him?"

"No," she replied.

By then the Sealdah station was visible and what she told us, we would never forget in our lives. She said, "Remember I told you that I was posted as a plainclothes policewoman at Sagar Mela?"

Indranil said, "Yeah, so!"

"Well," she continued, "My purse was stolen then! With it my identity card and money. It was my first job so I couldn't tell anyone!"

She paused a bit and then said, "Unfortunately, Inspector Chowdhury called me a couple of days later and asked, "Where is your identity card?"

"I was dumbfounded and couldn't say anything."

"Here it is!" he had replied, throwing down the purse on the table said. "Dolly the pickpocket was caught today, and they found it on her with your identity card! She would have used it and gone scot-free!" he continued. We were about to alight the train when she said, "By the way, do you know who my inspector is?"

"Who?" we enquired.

She turned and pointed to the drunk guy and said, "He!" She quickly turned around and said, "We are waiting for the next robbery! After all, we have to work undercover you know!"

Tinku was there to receive us. We were all soaking wet with

perspiration.

However, Mr. Bhattacharyya said, "This is the last meeting before we part ways!"

We had already divided the looted money from the robbery committed by Indranil, Mr. Bhattacharyya, and his goons and so we decided to part ways forever. I have since then lead a crime-free life as a devoted housewife!

****

CORPORATE SMOKING

Clouds of smoke hovered over this part of the corporate world. It was lunch time. The waiters were running from one table to another. The cash register was un-relentlessly churning out change. The "No Smoking" sign was distinctly forgotten. It was here where the corporate individuals sometimes fought their verbal duals, discussed strategies and ended feuds that originated from the corporate table. Animosity was disguised deftly in the form of jokes and hurled like missiles. Blue and white collared individuals sat side by side and chatted. It was here that Mr. Alfanso, the General Manager of Duncan and Bradstreet, the software giant joined me. I had just finished my last grub and lit one cigarette. It was his habit to stroll out of his chamber at lunch time and walk a block or two entirely on his own before having his lunch. Today was no exception. He was a man of short stature but commanded enormous respect. His intelligent eyes shone out of his rimless spectacles. The knot of his tie hung at the base of his chest and marked the crest of his pot belly. He was known fondly to all as "The Boss". His paternal attitude towards others marked him out from the rest of the management clan.

He occupied one chair just in front of me and placing his hands parallel to his torso over the clean white table interjected, "It's a hot day today, isn't it!"

I meekly nodded in agreement.

He continued, "This smoking sometimes gets on my nerves!"

I said, "I happen to be a smoker too!" as I revealed the glowing end of the long sleek white cigarette. Though at first, I was apprehensive about whether he was indirectly asking me to throw it away. But I puffed on thinking maybe I could get away.

Then he suddenly raised his arm and motioned at one of the waiters. What he asked next drove me down memory lane. It was a personal question.

He had enquired, "When did you have your first cigarette?"

I had replied, "Well, it was in class eleven I suppose. It was a day when nothing went right. My dog had died that evening and there was a lot of tension for my coming exams. Then one of my friends had offered one of these and said, "A puff or two and you will feel right, buddy!'"

"And you took it!" he said.

The waiter had then placed a plate of dosa in front of him.

"That was your first mistake." he said, before attacking the dosa with a fork.

Well, frankly does one individual keep a count of his mistakes that he makes in his life? I really wanted to ask him, if he ever did and somehow kept mum.

"And, the second one?"

"After graduation, when all my efforts were turning futile to find a suitable job, I started to smoke in the real sense. The lucky guys kept us well supplied."

"Nowadays, merit no longer seems to be the sole criteria for getting a job." he said.

I added, "Well, I almost starting believing it."

This pushed me back to that day when Mr. Alfanso was sitting across the table along with others and grilling me on the day of my interview. Well, circumstances were different then. The same person was now sitting across the table and having lunch with me.

"Tobacco is destroying today's youth." he said.

"I have tried to leave it a thousand times."

He smiled and added, "That reminded me of one incident. When I was small, my mother used to fast on some occasion or other. I tried to fast with her once or twice. What really happened was worth noting. Well, I used to fast till eleven or twelve in the afternoon and when hunger took the upper hand gobble some cashew nuts behind her back. Then again fast in the real sense, fast till two and then again have something. Again fast till four, and have something. And ultimately end fasting when my mom used to be tired of keeping me supplied with food. This was the attempt of fasting for the entire day."

I laughed and said, "I really enjoyed that!"

"Tobacco must be fought. It is destroying today's youth."

He continued, "You know all these beggars first get addicted to tobacco and then to smack and ultimately end up being thieves in order to support themselves. That's why the crime rate is spiralling up so rapidly."

I replied, "What an inference!"

Even though I didn't agree with him in entirety, I had to nod in agreement because of the poster that I had seen in his chamber when I entered it for the first time. It had the message

"**RULES** of surviving in the Corporate Jungle":

Rule 1: The Boss is always right.

Rule 2: Even if the boss is wrong, follow Rule 1."

From that day, I had practiced in earnestly.

He suddenly stopped eating looked at me and said, "But you must agree that smoking is enormously injurious to health. I was just going through this report that said that a young mother died of lung cancer leaving behind her three-year-old daughter."

I said, "Yes, women should be strictly forbidden to smoke".

He asked, "And why not men?"

"Passive smoking causes more problems. Children nowadays seem to develop asthma and other breathing problems. My neighbour's son has developed it too. I think the adults are responsible for it only." he added.

I had heard this on innumerable occasions but from Mr. Alfanso, I was probably the last person I could imagine. My lungs were aching for another dose of nicotine-laced fumes, but I couldn't help noticing the fanatical zeal with which Mr. Alfanso carried on. I had to resist from lighting another cigarette! I had to! The office forbade us from smoking in the office hours but this was the hour, which the smokers looked forward to just to have a puff or two. I really resisted my instincts.

"People became virtual slaves of cigarettes. They have to have one in the morning to create bowel pressure, I mean all those who suffer from constipation. One before lunch to enhance their appetite and one after lunch in fear that they don't lose their appetite! Then every now and then, they need a cigarette. Some people do it to reduce tension and frustration. They say it soothes the nerves."

"And I am one of them." I admitted.

Cigarette become bosses. I really do not think that they need one if you have one like me. Or do you?" he quipped.

I smiled and said, "Definitely not!"

He continued, "Have you noticed all the illegal temporary stalls that have cropped up. These actually are responsible for selling kids cigarettes. They even tap electricity illegally. They are destroying our kids too."

I asked, "Do they have a choice? With the state of employment to-day, if I didn't have this job, I may have been in their shoes too."

He said, "Then I would definitely have been your first customer."

I laughed at it.

"Today, I have noticed that the police have torn down all the illegal encroachments. Maybe some V.I.P is visiting".

He continued, "Where did you get that packet of cigarettes?"

I replied, "Nehru Place."

He said, "Oh, that's quite far off. I suppose you buy it while going home or while coming?"

"Anything that suits me," I replied.

The clock was fast approaching two and Mr. Alfanso suddenly realized it. The meeting was scheduled to start at quarter-to-two and Mr. Alfanso hastily waved at the waiter. The cafeteria was slowly getting empty. As the waiter brought the bill, he left a handsome tip and said, "Let's go"

We left the cafeteria and headed for the lift. As we entered the lift I noticed that Mr. Alfanso had pressed the button to the seventh floor. I was taken aback because the meeting was in the conference hall, which was on the fourth floor only. The terrace was on the seventh floor.

I inquisitively inquired, "The terrace?"

"Yes son, I need to say something to you in private." he said.

As the lift ascended, I started to get all sorts of weird ideas regarding this man was about to confide to me. Why could he not speak to me in his chamber? I had joined the job, and only two months had passed from the date of joining and was he displeased with my performance? Well, getting sacked from a fortune five hundred company was no big deal. I could feel drops of perspiration trickling down my neck. My insecurity had started to play havoc. I wished I had smoked another cigarette. As we reached the terrace, the vast expense of the corporate world hung around us in the shape of skyscrapers. The dreams of owning this empire one day were fast evaporating. My mouth was dry. Mr. Alfanso stepped out in the sun he threw his arms wide open and took a couple of deep breaths.

Then he glanced sideways and said, "Son, even if this is against everything. I really can't help it. I really have to do it before every board meeting. My wife even presented me with a new suite as promised but I really can't do it. These bloody policemen are responsible for this situation today. However, this should strictly remain between us!"

I looked at those clouded eyes and meekly nodded before uttering, "It will, Sir"

Thinking he was about to reveal some big corporate scandal out of guilt, I was tense. Whatever he said I really couldn't forget.

He said, "Give me one of those cigarettes, will you. I prefer that brand of yours, too!"

****

THE BACKDOOR ENTRY!

The policeman saluted and asked, "Why didn't you inform us earlier, Sir?"

My father, who towered over me at 6'2" was taken aback too. Without waiting for the answer, the policeman had hauled me up in his arms. Other colleagues of his, assisted my mom and sister. Some cleared the path hurriedly. I realized we were no longer anonymous figures among the thousands.

One of the cops had asked me "Where does your father work?"

I had replied, "He was an officer at…" but my parched voice had forced me to reply even more softly "the British Council." Strangely, my answer seemed to be lost in the mayhem of the children of the same god, who were still waiting in that chaotic queue that had proceeded some fifty meters in those last four hours.

After a thirty-six kilometre trek, we stood at the mouth of the Amarnath Caves. It was 12,000 feet above the sea level. Two amazing facts remain as memories of the journey. The cold would grip us and thrash us with its large tentacles when we stopped and when we started to move we would perspire out of exhaustion due to the treacherous terrain. The other remains the fact that made me realize the worth of food and water in the place.

I also remember that I had complained to my father of my feet being cold even though I was wearing two pairs of woollen socks and a pair of good mountaineering boots. My father had pointed out the fact that there was a small kid, younger than me who was trekking over the snow with only a pair of large socks! This is India and the power of faith! That had made me realize how fortunate people we were. These were the experiences, that made me the man that I am today.

The golden snow-capped peaks had shivered in the cascading rays of the new born sun and come crashing down on this world of mortals as the crystal-clear water. Moss had invaded where the conifers had given way. It was here where nature's beauty raced against its power of devastation. The wet earth underneath would sometimes give way taking horse and rider down the steep precipices.

"The Almighty's will," someone would say.

Someone else uttered, "The result of past sins." People then stealthily bypassed the tragedy. The single fact remained that the journey of the near and dear one's who were afflicted by this tragedy ended then and there.

Thousands waited ahead of us, to get a glimpse of Lord Shiva before the auspicious moments flew by. There even a nine-year-old boy like me had understood the power of money. Out of the hustling crowd of devotees, people held out currency notes above their heads and the very enforcers of law handpicked them. Unfortunately, there was neither Kiran Bedi nor Anna Hazare to look into it.

My father a man of principles had said, "If the Lord wishes to see us, He will."

However, when the police personnel had insisted, he had relented after taking a look at our faces. They had taken us to see the lord in what one may call the "backdoor entry!"

Then we saw what we had gone to seek. The petals, the milk, and the green fruit leaves had added colour to the lord. We were fortunate to be able to seek the blessing of the head priest too, courtesy the over-enthusiastic police men. We even managed to get the glimpse of the two holy pigeons the so-called messengers of Lord Shiva. The sudden change in the hospitality of the cops was amazing. They stood guarding our shoes when we entered the Amarnath caves whereas the shoes of the other devotees were strewn all over the place. They saluted us at the slightest pretext and even tried to humour us. When my father offered money, they retreated as if the sight of money would damn their souls to perdition. We were shocked at what seemed impossible for commoners like us.

In the late afternoon, we had returned to Panchtarani where we were camping for the night. We would assemble around the bonfire and have tea and biscuits. We were relating our experiences to each other and then we noticed Mr. Mishra the old bald gentleman, who was our father's colleague was coming along. It was six in the afternoon and almost four hours after all the other members of our trekking group had returned. Mr. Mishra's physical idiosyncrasy was characterized by a large potbelly. An equally impressive and large camera whose lens zoomed out of this large round physique. His obsession with photography had driven him to capture both nature and the lord through his lenses.

While sipping coffee he had confessed, "I have spoken a lie in this holy place!"

After taking another sip, the soft-spoken gentleman continued, "The lord be merciful enough to forgive me for it!" This was followed by a stunning silence. What followed next was even more amazing. He pointing to my father added, "I saw Mr. Dhar standing in the queue while most of the others took the easy way out. So all I did was tell the nearest policeman that that tall gentleman was the District Inspector General Police, of West Bengal!"

****

THE HEARING!

Litigation was the soul mate of Mr. Ramesh Chandra. Bold letters were embossed on the nameplate when you stood in front of his office door.

The name plate greeted "Ramesh Chandra Advocate, High Court"

Ramesh Chandra was an individual who knew the laws of the Indian Constitution better than the lines of his palm. The uncanny sixth sense and dynamic personality made him stand out from the rest. He was a self-made man, who fought his way up to his present position with neither money nor connections to help him. He had done so solely with his intellect and hard work. Now he worked for the rich for five days, searching for loopholes and flaws in the laws and made his money. Still he managed to keep in touch with his roots and devoted one day to helping the poor who came to his doorsteps to seek justice. He never failed them and fought these trials with the zeal of a fundamentalist. He would put in seventy hours a week and age didn't seem to slow him down. Friday was a very busy day and the lesser fortunate milled at his office. Mr. Chandra would direct the junior lawyers who had just been out of the law colleges, to handle these cases.

He would tell the budding lawyers, "You will have to stick around. Handle each case and learn a few courtroom tricks. Prosecuting is an art and you have to perfect this art. Maybe one day you will be in my shoes too."

One Friday one of these junior assistants brought a case to his notice. It was a case where a young man had come to seek redressal against the illegal occupancy of a house by the goons of a certain political party. The first information report, as reported to the police were of no use, since the police were working with the goons too. The helpless eyes of the youth named Sumit instilled a sense of pity in Mr. Chandra. Hence, he decided to handle the case himself. He instructed his personal assistant to give Sumit an appointment since it was already past eight in the evening. Clapping Sumit's back, Mr. Chandra left saying, "Don't worry, I will take care of it!"

The little ray of hope alluded by this circumstantial encouragement by so great a man to hear his case instilled a sense of jubilation in Sumit. He went home with renewed hope. Next morning he arrived at the office of Mr. Chandra with the resolve of throwing the goons out. Unfortunately, this time, he found that he had forgotten to take an appointment in his jubilation and found that he couldn't go past the receptionist who said, "No one is allowed without a valid appointment." On Monday, he got the same response. The next day was no different. Friday came along and again he got his chance when he managed an appointment for the next Thursday. As the days flew by, his expectation began to web. He, however, didn't lose his resolve yet! Somehow the no hope situation was cropping out of somewhere. Hope was the last resort and that made life worth living, and he earnestly clutched to it.

Thursday came along, however Mr. Chandra was found wanting, as he had flown to Amritsar to attend the inauguration of a hospital for the poor. The day's appointments were shifted by a week. The first signs of frustration were appearing on the distant horizon. Did poor guys like Sumit have a way out? On the scheduled day Sumit arrived only to find Mr. Chandra leaving since the great lawyer's son had reported ill. He had failed again. Sumit realized that appointments were of no use! Desperation forced him to think otherwise. Monday ushered in a new week, and Sumit decided to meet the advocate by hook or by crook. He went and waited the whole day outside the advocate's office but to no avail. He couldn't get past the stubborn secretary. Yet, he would not leave this undone. As Mr. Chandra was leaving the office premises in his car, Sumit dashed in front on it waving his hands to stop it. The security guard reacted fast and ran out mistaking him to be some miscreant. The guard caught hold of him and pinned him down. This drama had caught the attention of the advocate and he instructed the guard to leave him alone.

Mr. Ramesh pointing a finger to Sumit said, "You come here!"

Sumit brushed himself off and went up to his car.

Mr. Ramesh said, "Son you remind me of my youth!" He quickly jotted down a telephone number on the back of his card with his pen. Handling over his card he said, "Call me tomorrow and let's see what I can do for you."

A couple of rings and the advocate was online the next morning.

Sumit meekly mumbled, "Sir, I am the guy who stopped your car yesterday."

"Yeah, I am supposed to inaugurate a primary school at Hosiarpur next Tuesday. You are welcome to accompany me there and I can hear your case in the spare time. Is that ok with you son? That's the earliest that I can give you, otherwise I will have to cancel some appointment to accommodate you, which is really not feasible for the time being." It sounded like a command to Sumit.

Sumit replied, "As you wish, Sir. Thank you, Sir!"

"Come over to my place at say around seven in the morning and tell the security guard your name. This time I hope he will not pin you down!" saying this he laughed out aloud. Sumit didn't know what to say so he kept quiet.

"By the way, try to be punctual son!" said Mr. Ramesh before the receiver went dead.

On Tuesday morning, Sumit arrived sharp at seven in the morning at the "Chandra Villa" located in the posh south extension locality. The white mansion had a different aura around it. The guard let him in. Neatly trimmed hedges surrounded the green carpet of grass on the lawn and creepers adorned the walls. Bonsai hung beside the Corinthian pillars and magnified the balcony. He was ushered in by the servant and was offered a seat in the gorgeously decorated drawing room. It was a room fit for the kings. He was awe-struck by the richness of the colours that adorned the place.

Two gentlemen were sitting on the fur sofa. They were sipping tea and chatting. Mr. Chandra arrived shortly and shook hands with these gentlemen.

Mr. Chandra then asked Sumit, "What would you like Tea or Coffee?"

Sumit politely said, "No, Thank you! I don't have the habit of taking tea or coffee!"

Turning towards the gentlemen he said, "Well, since this young man appears to be filled, we can leave!"

One of them said, "Why not!"

They started for Hosiarpur almost immediately in the car that these gentlemen had brought with them. Sumit was asked to sit in front as these two gentlemen and Mr. Chandra occupied the back seat. Sumit was bored throughout the entire journey. All he did was sit and watch the dry countryside as the car trudged along slowly avoiding the potholes. The parched dry earth exploded with heat. The dry barren trees appeared to spread their branches towards the sky as if to pray for some rain.

The Bitumen road ended and gave way to an unpaved road as the scorching sun beat against the roof of the car. Without an A.C, it was more like a furnace. Mr. Chandra was too very preoccupied to even talk to Sumit. Sumit could make head or tail of their conversation. He realized he had to bear the whims of the great lawyer. There was no way out. The entire day revolved around the inauguration. Sumit watched, as one speaker followed another, one speech followed another, each earnestly trying to outdo the other, by glorifying the great advocate amidst their presence.

"Acts of such benevolence are rare!" said one.

"Kindness even greater!" said another, as the advocate basked in the glory of the praises showered on him. The temperature rose as did Sumit's temper. He was thinking what use was it to accompany a man who really couldn't spare a minute for him. Sumit ate alone and unrecognized, unwanted in one corner during lunch. It was commoners and non-entities like Sumit who created heroes out of common individuals and followed them as slaves following a master. Strange are the ways of the world. After all, justice is fair they say!

Finally, around six in the evening, Mr. Ramesh bid adieu to Hosiarpur amidst much fanfare. Children ran after the car as it slowly vanished into the horizon leaving a trail of clouded dust behind. It was then that Sumit got his chance to speak. Sumit and Mr. Chandra sat side by side as the chauffeur drove the car. The advocate listened patiently with his head resting on the car's back seat's back-rest. It was a long story. After sometime, Sumit noticed the advocate had closed his eyes. He still continued. Doubts crept up inside his mind. Was the great man listening to his discourse? He stopped suddenly, as suspicion took the upper hand. He noticed deep breaths disseminating the silence as the car trudged along slowly. He had not even reached the halfway mark and the advocate had fallen asleep! He brought his face close to the advocate's face but was greeted with silence. Sumit couldn't rein in the devil called frustration. He looked out of the window and cursed silently. Then he couldn't control his instincts from blurting out, "The bastard fell asleep!"

The chauffeur heard it. He glanced sideways and smiled. Yet, he continued driving without a word. Around half eight, the car rolled on the porch of the "Chandra Villa." Mr. Chandra woke up. His little daughter ran to greet he father. Sumit was too very frustrated. He started to leave. Then suddenly, Mr. Chandra said, "Son, I didn't hear your entire story!"

Sumit looked back. He wanted to hurl back all the abuses he knew. But after all, he was just a commoner, who had come to seek justice under Ramesh Chandra the famous advocate. He was thinking that it was a mistake on approaching Mr. Chandra in the first place. Seeking justice by becoming a lawyer seemed much easier than running after advocates who seemed to give dates for hearing and nothing else. He felt sick. Yet, strangely he followed Mr. Ramesh to his study.

The study was filled with thick books. Files and papers were stacked on one side of the computer. There was hardly any space to sit as even the chairs were occupied by books and files. Mr. Chandra removed some files from a chair and let Sumit sit. He occupied the revolving chair on the other end of the table and faced Sumit. He said, "You may start with the case details!"

Sumit with almost tears in his eyes quizzed him, "From where do I start?"

The advocate smiled and replied, "From where the bastard fell asleep!"

****

SWOLLEN KNUCKLES

Dropsy faces thrust out of the windows. The buses were jam-packed. Crowds of people walked alongside the inching traffic towards the Howrah Station. The still tropical atmosphere added monotony to the inching traffic. Perspiration welled out and flowed down incessantly. Each motorist tried to out-manoeuvre each other in that narrow space. They only ended up adding to the chaotic confluence of unruly vehicles. Smoke emissions choked the traffic further and it choked and spitted its way through the bridge. Each man wanted to reach home a little quicker trying to escape the hassles of the snail-paced traffic and each made elementary mistakes leading to further delays. Many had trains to catch, so each hurried on impatiently.

Suddenly, a man in one of the buses seemed to crane his neck to have a better look through the window. He tried to have a sniff of the cool wind flowing from the Ganges. For quite a long time he seemed to stare at something.

Suddenly, breaking his reverie he excitedly pointed out and yelled, "Look! Look!"

Almost instantaneously, most of the passengers looked out trying to see what he was trying to show. Someone unable to follow his finger yelled out, "What? What is it?"

Then another passenger more perturbed shouted, "There, there it is!"

The man beside him enquired, "Where? Where?"

Just then, the traffic woke up with a jerk and made a sudden jolt forward as the driver slammed the accelerator. The jolt threw many of the passengers out of balance and added to the increasing tantrum. The man who first shouted added, "The truck! The truck!"

When the traffic again came to a jolting halt the truck had become the cynosure of all eyes. The scrutiny suddenly began. The light-brown coloured truck was nothing of interest except it carried soil and loam which was evident as loose lumps of loam tumbled out on occasional jerks.

Then someone said, "The hand! The hand!"

It was then that one noticed that a greased hand sticking out of the loose loam. Those swollen knuckles spoke for themselves. The thought of it would have sent shivers down many a spine.

One of the passengers yelled out, "Stop it! Stop it!"

His actions caught the attention of the pedestrians who were separated from the traffic by steel railing. They caught up in a frenzy. One suddenly jumped across the railing and stopped the car trailing the truck.

The youth yelled, "Stop it! Stop it!"

The equally puzzled car driver slammed the brake as the traffic, which had just started forward came to a grinding halt, stopping all vehicles following it. The traffic behind the car expressed their anger by blaring the horns as loudly as they could.

The owner occupying the seat next to the driver of the car enquired, "Why? Why the hell?"

The youth countered, "Because I ordered you!"

By then someone else shouted, "Not the car! The Truck! Fool, the truck!"

Someone else added in the chorus yelling at the top of his voice, "Yes, the truck! The truck!"

The man who had gallantly stopped the car now fled towards the truck, leaving behind the cursing occupants of the car, as the focus changed.

More people jumped over the railing and joined the pursuit, as few passengers from the bus alighted and started for the truck too.

Strangely, in the resulting mayhem, the truck driver sensing something was very wrong stopped the truck, jumped down and fled. After all, the public was chasing him. Getting caught would mean sure death or severe beating. Strangely, he too managed to drown himself in the sea of pedestrians who walked towards the Howrah station. Almost instantly, someone managed to reach the truck. The man who reached the truck asked the guy following him, "Now what?"

The later advised, "Let the others arrive!" not knowing why they had stopped the truck. Then someone who knew the exact purpose of the chase reached and pointed to the "Swollen Knuckles". Then someone bravely climbed up and dropped on his knees and started digging with his bare hands. Others followed, still others watched curiously. A sea of humanity with their endless compassion surrounded the truck and the traffic was given the right dose of anaesthesia.

"What people! Murdering a man and transporting him under mud!" said a voice from the crowd. Another added, "Crime never pays!"

Someone said, "The stench is not there, may have been done within an hour or so!"

An old man who pushed his way through the crowd said, "What is the use of all this when brave and gallant youth of today couldn't even catch a mere truck driver!"

One among the younger generation countered, "Grandpa, why didn't you do it yourself?"

The toothless man glared and boomed out, "If I was a young man like you, I would have certainly done it!" Then he repeated, "What good for nothing are these dynamic youth of today? Couldn't even catch the bastard!"

The swollen brownish fingers continued to gape out of the soil. By now the man who had made his astonishing discovery had reached and under his protégé a section of the crowd was getting a first-hand account of the action they had missed. Such occurrences rarely do happen and seldom should they be missed.

One individual in the crowd who happened to be a photographer was silently regretting the fact that he had left his camera in his studio and silently vowing never to go without it in the near future. Such a scoop would have the fourth estate henchmen eating out of his hands. A hand, protruding out of the truck, transporting loam! Men on their knees, desperately digging with their bare hands! A better angle could have been achieved, had he managed to stand at a higher elevation. The roof of the car following the truck would have been perfect. Yet, now all he could do was to watch it go.

Suddenly, someone among the crowd whipped out a cell-phone and suggested, "Why should we not inform the police!"

Another voice from the crowd added, "What can the police do now?"

"Is it not your duty to report it?" he fired back.

Yet another added, "Let me speak," as the other gentleman punched the numbers.

Suddenly one among the crowd spoke, "Look! Look!"

The attention again diverted back to the hand. It was strange but true that the hand seemed on longer swollen but it had shrivelled down suddenly. The more they removed the soil the more it got shrivelled. It didn't take them long to realize that the swollen hand was nothing more than an old soiled workman's glove made of buffalo leather with some loam, hay and air trapped in it!

****

IN SEARCH OF PEACE!

It was the 2nd of November. It was the day of the "All Souls Day." That evening when I was strolling, I found a young lady sitting on the tomb of the grave, in the cemetery.

I had asked hoarsely, "What are you doing here?"

The moment she turned, I realized that she was no more than a teenager, maybe. The drying remnants of the sun showed me that her eyes were red and sore from crying. I thought her expressive sad eyes must have been perfected enough by God to appeal to all humanity.

Then she answered, in her low tone, "I am searching for peace, in life or in death."

I didn't know what to say and the light of the lantern, which was placed beside her flickered and danced as our only hope in this dark cemetery.

She appeared to be a Muslim, as her hijab was dishevelled. Her once beautiful black hair was slowly drifting in the wind.

I slowly sat beside her.

After a while I asked, "Where are you from?"

"Aleppo"

"Where is it?"

"Aleppo, Syria!"

"Never heard of it! Is it near Baghdad?"

"Not Baghdad, but Damascus."

"Yes."

"How could you have come this far?"

"I fled!"

"Why?"

"I couldn't take it anymore."

"Well, what about your family?"

"My mom died in a bomb blast in Aleppo when I was fourteen. I never saw my father! I had a younger brother and a sister. When the rebels came and seized Aleppo, my sister was married to one of the rebels and I was auctioned off to the Arabs! I don't know what happened to my brother. They sold me off to a Sheikh in Dubai, who presented me to his Tamil business partner, who brought me here. I fled when I found the chance. I know this man is afraid of ghosts so, I am hiding in the cemetery!"

"Are you not afraid of ghosts?"

She answered, "I have seen people dying, when the bombs split open their limbs! When my mom died, I mean when the bomb fell on her, she was returning from the market with some milk for my younger brother! The bomb fell, and her body was blown to bits so much so that her one of her eyes splintered out of her skull and fell inside our house on the floor beside the cot where I was studying, and the second floor building came crashing down due to the impact of the bomb! Can I ever be afraid after what I went through?"

Big drops of tears were flowing from her eyes.

Then she asked with her quivering voice, "Who are you?"

I replied, "I am the custodian of this Cemetery."

"Dying is easier for me than to die each moment I live! Are you a Christian?"

"Yes!"

"Will you turn me in?"

"Should I?"

"I don't know! Don't you hate me because I am a Muslim?"

I looked at her and replied, "Do you hate me if I am a Christian?"

She intensely looked at my eyes and replied, "I don't know?"

"Why?"

"The ISIL rebels said it's is the Americans who blew up my mom with their bombs, when they married off my sister! They had said the people who killed my mom were Christians. But it's they who chained me up and auctioned me to the Arab Sheikh, who tortured me!"

"Do you believe them now?"

"I don't know!"

"What's your name?"

"Salma"

As the shroud of darkness enveloped the cemetery, and the wind slowly started to howl, I thought, I should help her out.

I commanded, "Come with me will you!"

We walked past the Dutch tomb stones and headed towards my dilapidated den. I knew she would be safe there for the night.

We went inside and seeing the rooms in tatters made no difference to her. The thin red bricks of the outhouse which was now my residence, gapped outside exposing the old plastered wall. The red cemented floor had turned grey. I had offered her some water to drink which she slowly began to drink. It soothed her nerves, I guess.

She slowly removed her Hijab, as I saw her beautiful face. She would be hardly nineteen or at most twenty.

She asked me, "Is it true that there are ghosts around here?"

I smiled and replied, "Well, there is a lot of history to this cemetery. Even if you find the ghosts, they are either speaking Dutch, Portuguese or English. They are not native Indians like me. This is a Protestant Dutch Cemetery. The cemetery is a small, square plot enclosed with high walls within which are the tombs. The tombs are either flat, dome and pyramid shaped as you can see! Occasionally they have been diversified by broken pillars, urns and sarcophagi, now all of them are more of less blackened by exposure of the sun, wind and the rain. The grass is wild here, and there you will find bushes of a beautiful orange flowered weed that infests these parts of the country! You will find one or two descendants of the British, Portuguese or Dutch who would descend here in search of the tomb of their ancestors! But you are safe here."

She had asked, "What is your name?"

"Well, you can call me Mr. Hope."

She asked, "What about your family, Mr. Hope?"

"Family! Well, I was born here, just like my father, who too was born here just like his father!"

She smiled at this joke.

I continued, "Well, I was married to Angela Lawson. She borne me a son and a daughter. My daughter Mary passed away at the age of two, due to diarrhoea. She would be of your age by now, I guess. I am not good with dates you know! My son, Andrew drowned while swimming in these backwaters here. He was nineteen then. Angela died of grief! I only thought my grief was unsurmountable. But your experience speaks volumes of your stamina, to face this devil called grief!"

Salma eyes had moistened up. She had kind eyes just like Angela, my wife.

As the wind howled, the tattered wooden remains of slats of the jalousie windows clattered in the wind. The flame of the old lantern flickered on.

Salma said, "It is getting cold in here."

"It is always cold in here. Would you like some more coffee?"

"Yes, please. That's really kind of you."

"Kindness? Do you think there is kindness left in this world?"

She kept quiet for some time.

Then she replied, "Well then, what's the way out?"

"I don't know!"

The cold wind again howled, and the wooden remains of the rickety door slammed shut. The wooden slats of the jalousie windows squeaked and cried out with the wind. We could still see the lantern placed on the tomb stone where I had found Salma sitting though the remains of the door.

Salma asked, "Don't these ghosts harm you."

I smiled and replied, "Well, they are ghosts of chivalrous men, who were gentlemen who died fighting with swords and cannons. They are not the ones who fight with deception and cowardice, or drop bombs on innocent people. I belong to those people who fought own duels!"

Salma smiled at this.

Salma now picked up the TIME Magazine that was kept beside the tattered bed. It had the picture of a decorated army general. She looked at it intensely and then said, "Why do people go to war?"

"My dear Salma, it is often said it is one of the most difficult question. People go in war due to hatred and greed. There are war on grounds of religion, on grounds of nationalism. Well nationalism pits men into hating men and killing them too. It is destroying the rationality of sanity and they end up killing other people whom they have never met. The same human blood is lost when there is war. Somewhere down the line, humanity loses out."

"But why are people decorated for killing other humans! Look all nations decorate the most aggressive soldiers who they term as warriors!"

"Well that's the funny part of it. Some say if you want peace then prepare for war! Mostly, innocent people get nothing out of it. It is an economic burden for nations. Do you think the heads of states do not understand this? Some say it helps to eliminate evil. We commit an evil deed of war to kill an evil. You cannot eliminate an evil by using an evil means. Love can eliminate evil and hatred. Most people may not agree with this, because this is a very difficult proposition. Moreover, there is no one point path to sure shot success since this issue is too complex."

Salma replied, "You appear to be a die-hard romantic, even at this age."

I smiled back wryly.

Suddenly Salma said, "Do you hear that?"

I said, "What?"

"Listen carefully!" replied Salma.

I smiled and then replied, "Don't be afraid Salma, I think they are rumbling in their graves, they usually do! They are otherwise harmless!"

Salma's concerned face actually reflected her fear!

Then I heard a noise that seemed like metal hitting stone. I got up and said to Salma, "Wait, don't go out of here! I think there are grave diggers searching for hidden treasure. I have to prevent them." Then I rushed out with my heavy pistol.

The howling of wind had picked up and it had started to drizzle. I picked up the lantern and went towards the direction of the noise. I could see two men digging the grave. I howled like a wolf and charged towards them. I could feel the platoon of soldiers consisting of the Dutch, Portuguese and the British chasing them in unison. As if they had risen out of their graves to assist me. I ran as far as I could chase them till I reached the gate of the cemetery. They had left and ran away shouting, "Ghost! Ghost!"

Then I went back to inspect the spot. I found that they had vandalized the grave. They had dug up the grave and I found they had left behind the gold platted coffin. Beside the coffin, I found a small familiar looking box. I now realized what they were after. So I took the box and started for my den. The drizzle had picked up and I could feel the cold dampness reaching my bones. I was dead sure they would not return that night after the fright I must have had given them. I felt dead tired and felt I had not slept of so long.

I could see Salma's white face peeping in fright from behind the door. I put down the lantern and placed the hefty pistol beside my rickety broken wooden door.

I smiled and replied, "Bloody grave diggers! Fled on

confrontation, crying ghost!"

I smiled and handed over the small box and said to her, "I think they were searching for this. I think you need it more than me."

My cold wet shaking hand, had touched her extended hands. I could feel she too was shivering. I didn't know if she was shivering with fright or coldness. I assured her however saying, "Don't worry as long as I am there. There is nothing to worry!"

I had a feeling that my task of protecting the graves so had reached a point of culmination. I had handed Salma what she needed most.

She asked, "What do you think is in this?"

I smiled wryly and told her, "Well, I don't think there will the treasures of seven kings! But hopefully enough to get you started!"

Her bewildered eyes said it all.

She then asked, "Can I open it, now?"

I said, "Keep it with you. Open it tomorrow, at day break. By the way, you can sleep here in this bed!"

She asked, "And you?"

I had replied, "Well, I don't sleep at night. I am the custodian, and you know after what happened tonight, I have to be extra cautious!"

That night I roamed aimlessly around the cemetery. Inspecting all the graves and throwing the dead flowers away from the tomb stones. It was almost day-break when I returned to my den and found Salma still sleeping soundly like a baby, yet she was clutching the small box to her breast like a baby clutches her doll. Then I tipped toed to the other room, which was once my son, Andrew's room and slowly occupied the cot and fell asleep. The room had almost caved in, however, my rickety bone felt no pain. After all, I too had been searching for some peace for so long.

The next morning, when Salma woke up, she didn't find Mr. Hope in the outhouse. She was so hungry that she left the cemetery and went in search of some food. She did beg for some food and the got two bananas from the street vendor. She ate one and started to return towards the cemetery. She found that there was a crowd of people waiting outside the gates of the cemetery.

When she enquired, "What's the matter?"

One of the guys replied, "One of the graves of Mrs. Angela Hope has been vandalized and desecrated! The authorities of the Southern Church of India who looks after the cemetery must be informed. The caretaker of the cemetery, Mr. Jim Davis found out this morning."

Salma was a bit alarmed by this, but she asked, "Are the descendants' of the Hope family somewhere here?"

The man laughed and replied, "You must be crazy, Angela Hope died long back in the eighteenth century. Her husband's grave Captain Raymond Hope's grave is just situated beside her grave.

They were the only Anglo-Indian members who were buried here! You got to get crazy trying to trace any of them!"

Salma alarmed at this didn't say anything more and walked to Ernakulam which was around six km from the Dutch cemetery of Fort Kochi. Tears were flowing down her eyes! She kept reminding herself to remain strong! Then she begged her way to Cochin. On reaching Cochin, she had opened the box. She found two small diamonds in the size of pigeon eggs and an old parchment. What was scribbled on the parchment was beyond her imagination. It read, "Dear Angela, May these diamonds sparkle and add happiness to you, in life and in death. May you find peace!" Much to her amazement, the part of the name Angel was stuck off from the name Angela and instead Salma was scribbled over it.

Salma sold off one of the diamonds and started a new life in Cochin. She is now married to a Hindu tailor named Gunusekharan. She named her son as Hope. However, on the All Soul's day, she makes it a point to visit the Dutch Cemetery in Fort Kochi and leave a candle and a bouquet of flowers for the Hope Family. If someone asks her why she visits she would answer, "Well, they were the ancestors of my long lost friend Mary Hope, from Syria." She was now at peace with herself. No one has even heard of ghosts or paranormal activities from the Dutch Cemetery after that, which was once vandalized. Neither did they find the grave diggers!

****

FEAR!

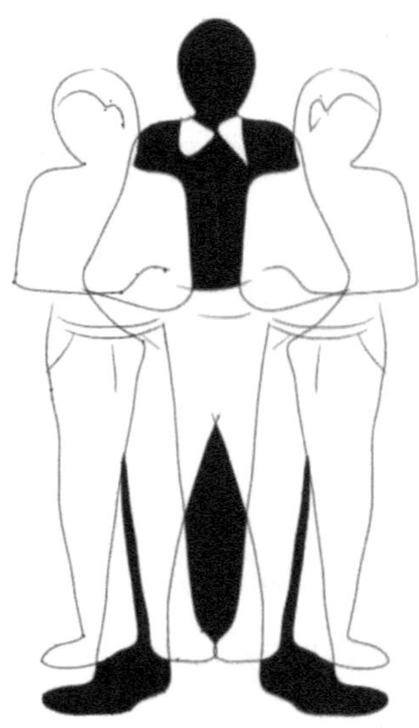

When I was about eight years old, my father forced me to go with him to the funeral of a friend of his that I didn't know. I had unwillingly relented. We were living at Nainital at that time. At that tender age, I was a shy kid. I was more intent to play games than to go and visit a funeral. I loathed it but had to listen to my father.

It was a clear morning, when we got there. We had parked our car outside the cemetery. The cemetery had a narrow gravelled pathway and on both sides of the pathway. It was dotted with Cedar, Spruce, Cypress and Miranda trees which acted as a canopy for the underlying graves. We had walked along the path towards the congregation where the ceremony was to take place. I stayed in a corner beside a Cypress tree waiting for the time to pass and then again was peeping at the proceedings of the ceremony to check if it was over. Then suddenly, a man approached me from behind and said, "Enjoy life boy, be happy because time flies, look at me now, I didn't enjoy life!" It was a weird stray comment from a stranger. Then he passed his hand over my head and his hands kissed my hair and then he left as mysteriously as he had arrived. My father, before leaving, forced me to say goodbye to the dead person. "When I looked in the coffin, I was startled that the man who was talking to me when I was standing beneath the Cypress tree was the same man in the Coffin." I was petrified and yet when my father asked, "You ok!" I had somehow answered, "Yes!"

Although, I had sweaty palms, I didn't have the courage to tell him about the incident. After all it was broad day light and I didn't want to make myself the laughing stock. Silently I had suffered unable to tell anyone of this incident. For several years later, when my father passed away, I went to the same cemetery. After his burial, as we were walking towards my car, with my mother beside me. Then again, I saw the man. The man who was my father's friend, whom they had buried at the cemetery when I had visited this place years ago, was walking out of the crowd and walked towards me. The stress and everything got to me and I fainted petrified. When I came around, I didn't find the dead man, and the first words that I had uttered was, "The man in the coffin!" "Yes, that was your father, Johnny!" replied my mom. "No not him, I saw one of my father's dead friends!" The shock is tremendous, I guess!" replied my mom and stared at my girlfriend Joanna. I had not elaborated after that. Neither did they ask me anything regarding this anymore. I was not able to sleep properly and had repeated nightmares. I was terrified of being alone. I didn't turn off the light at night and had several other turmoil which almost wrecked me psychologically. I always wanted to know, "Why me? "Later on, I was forced to visit many psychologists at the behest and insistence of my mother and girlfriend. Though they said, "There is no issues with me!" This process went on for two decades. Then I discovered something incredible that changed my life, completely. That dead idiot had an identical twin brother.

∗∗∗∗∗∗∗∗∗∗∗∗∗∗∗∗∗∗∗∗∗∗∗∗∗∗∗∗∗∗∗∗∗

THE PECULIAR TRIBE CALLED LAWYERS

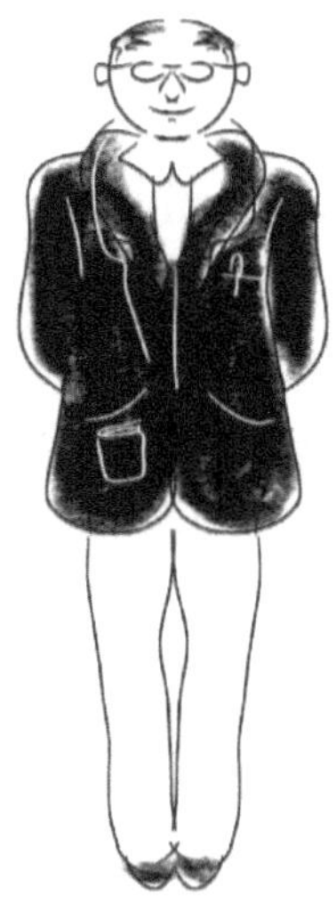

It was January 1974, and it was past noon when Poritosh Sarkar stepped inside his rented three-storied house at Maniktala, Kolkata. Poritosh was dressed neatly in a white shirt and white trousers. He had left his black overcoat at the lawyers' cabin. He had a subdued look on his face and he didn't know what to say to his wife Poroma since he knew his purse and pen was missing on his way home from the court. He distinctly remembered bumping into a young man while alighting from the tram near Maniktala. He had almost cursed the man, who seemed to be in a hurry to get on the tram.

Poritosh, had the opinion that, "Everyone who was charged in the name of law, needed a lawyer to defend himself." He had developed the uncanny habit of representing the petty criminals, pickpockets and small time criminals.

Poroma on realizing that something was wrong had asked, "What is it? You look so sad."

Poritosh meekly replied, "Well, I can't find my pen and purse."

On hearing this Poroma replied, "We all know that people have to suffer from the consequences of their acts sometime or the other. Defend more pickpockets and criminals and see what you get in return!"

Poritosh was not expecting this. Although, he knew his wife would be angry, so he kept quiet. Soon his elder brother's wife and his spinster sister also joined his wife and started making fun of the entire issue. Poristosh ate his lunch in silence and went to sleep in his room. He tossed and turned, he didn't get any sleep and finally got up when it was evening. He went in search of Kalu the pickpocket, who he had defended and had gone scot free last month.

Kalu was getting ready for his nocturnal outing when Poritosh confronted him. Kalu was a dark complexioned short man, yet he was very strong and had a twisted nose. His veins were all visible in his strong bare hands. His unkempt hair and his shoddy half shirt spoke of his sorry state of affairs. Poritosh said, "Well, this is the last time I have defended you. If I don't get my pen and purse back which was pickpocketed from me today afternoon, I am not going to represent anyone of you guys anymore!"

Kalu, not accustomed to threats didn't know how to react. Usually, his personality intimidated others. The fear of not being represented by a good lawyer at such a marginal fee, sank in! Then his gratitude towards Poritosh appeared suddenly as he said, "Sirji, please come with me, I will see what I can do!"

Then Kalu took Poritosh to Rajabazar moving from one dingy looking lane to another. Kalu went in and asked Poritosh to follow. They were then confronted by a hefty looking man possibly some henchman, who spoke in a quiet tone to Kalu. The man seemed agitated on seeing Poritosh, but he let them pass when Kalu insisted, "I have to meet Salim bhai, it's urgent!"

When Poritosh and Kalu entered the house, they found that it had red cemented courtyard. At the center of the courtyard sat a dark complexioned man in his forties on a cane chair, who had a grayish white beard and was smoking a cigarette. His hair had a frayed look. He was wearing bangles on his left hand. Poritosh was a bit taken aback, since he had successfully defended this man, a couple of months ago, whom Kalu now referred to as Salim. Poritosh remembered that Salim was referred to as Pintu when he was being ushered in the court of law, and it is surprising that the same fellow was now being referred to as Salim. Kalu had started relating what had happened to Poritosh, but then suddenly Poritosh interjected saying, "Hey, is your name Salim or Pintu?"

To this question Salim smiled and replied, "Well, we have many names, Sirji! I am originally Muslim and in India, most Muslims have a Hindu pet name as well. People who are close to me call me Salim and yet I have multiple other names which the police call as alias!"

Then Poritosh went on to relate what had happened and when he finished Kalu added, "Sirji, is saying that if he doesn't get back his pen and purse he will not defend anyone of us!"

Salim looked at Poritosh and said, "Well, although most people think that low scum of the society like us, do not have any ethics, but frankly we maybe pickpockets, thieves or low criminals but we have some code of conduct as well." Then he stopped and looked at Kalu and said, "We are not supposed to dupe our own brothers or people who can actually defend us! I will see what we can do!"

Kalu afterward accompanied Poritosh to the Rajabazar crossing and then left him alone. Poritosh decided to walk back home, pondering whether what he had just done was correct or not! Or was he getting sucked into the vortex of crime. It was nine when he reached home and was confronted by his elder brother Sanjay who said, "Well, I told you not to defend these criminals and now see what has happened. It is like a keeping a black cobra as a pet and feeding it with milk and then when it grows up, it starts biting its own owner. People like you will never learn!"

Kamala his brother's wife added, "Dada there is no point wasting time, money and energy after these petty criminals. You should stick to defend rich clients who can give you more fame and reputation than these lowly idiots. You should stick to more affluent clients."

Poritosh wanted to say, "I defend them because they are human beings like me. They are down-trodden and don't get opportunities like the common men. If someone is a proven thief, then people do not trust them anymore and they don't get even menial jobs. I think they deserve better. After all, to err is human!" However, strangely his voice was lost in the face of reasoning from almost all the family members of his.

The next evening, when Poritosh was returning home from the court, he found Kalu waiting for him at the entrance of the lane where he lived at Maniktala. Kalu promptly said, "Sirji, please follow me, Salim had asked me to inform you." Again, Kalu took Poritosh to Rajabazar and this time he went to that same dingy lane. This time he was confronted with a woman, who on recognizing Kalu let them through! On entering the house they found sprawled across the red cemented floor was around thirty to thirty five purses and an around 15 to 20 pens of different makes and designs.

Slowly Poritosh inspected and picked up his purse and pen from among the lot. The money in his purse was intact and the pen which was a gold nib parker was soon back in Poritosh's pocket. Poritosh said, "How did you get all these together so fast?"

"We have resources for these, I guess!" replied Salim with raised shoulders .

"We won't let you go so easily, Mr. Sarkar! We need good lawyers as well!" said Kalu.

Then, Mr. Poritosh returned home jubilant. It was around nine when he entered home and shouted, "I have retrieved my purse and pen. I think I wouldn't have retrieved my purse and pen had I only catered to rich clients!"

After that, Mr. Poritosh defended the so-called scum of the society with equal zeal. I guess, such passion is only attributable to the peculiar tribe known as lawyers.

****

CORRUPTION SAVES THE DAY!

It was a clear morning when Mr. Ramprakash Ahuja set out for the Jairampur cemetery which was six kilometres from the Jairampur town. It was the cemetery where Mr. Ramprakash's grandfather Mr. Shivlal Ahuja was buried. Mr. Ramprakash was a small time business man settled in Kolkata, West Bengal. It was the last dying wish of Mr. Ramprakash's father Mr. Charulal Ahuja, that had brought him to this cemetery in the Changlang district of Arunachal Pradesh. The Jairampur cemetery was around one and half hour drive from Miao and around 25 kilometres from the Pangsan Pass of the Indo-Myanmar border. The cemetery is famous because it contains the tombstones of the allied soldiers, the Chinese and the Indian soldiers who fought side by side against the Japanese occupation and perished in the World War II. Many localities and labourers who were Hindus could also be found buried besides the graves of the martyred soldiers. It was an old cemetery, dilapidated with trees and thick undergrowth spilling over the tombstones. Mr. Ramprakash had trouble in locating his grandfather's tombstone at first, as the damp moss had covered the tombstone, but his efforts did not go in vain as he finally managed to locate his father's wish of giving a tribute to his late grandfather who was a soldier of the British Empire by offering a bouquet of flowers. Once the task was completed, he left the spooky place once and for all.

It was time for him to return to Miao. There he had his lunch and roamed about the picturesque town and saw a number of angling spots on the river Noa-Dehing. Then he went to catch a bus for the Mohanbari Airport of Dibrugarh, via Tinsukia from where he had an air-ticket to return to Kolkata. The road meandered through the lush green evergreen forest along the river then it went up the hills which are covered by a carpet of green foliage. The greenery flouted it produce of oxygen and after a sharp drizzle, the fresh green earth smelled so good. The psithurism was so beautiful to hear as the wind rushed across his face and hair as he occupied the window seat of the almost empty bus. The dusk had just set in and the green foliage turned a wee bit darker in shade as the darkness from hell enveloped the forest and the road. The bus trudged along slowly avoiding potholes.

Suddenly, he noticed the shrieks of a group of hoolock gibbons and one of them agitatedly emerged and disappeared in the undergrowth. The shadows were lengthening and then suddenly the driver cursed and the bus shrieked to a halt. A single large log was placed horizontally across the road. Then out of the shadows emerged the danger. Four to five armed men possibly dacoits boarded the bus as two-three others watched the proceeding from outside. On finding the bus empty, they cursed and threatened and heckled their way towards Mr. Ramprakash.

They ordered, "Give all you got or pay the price!"

Then they took his only gold wedding ring and whatever cash they could find on him. Thankfully they left behind the debit and credit cards he was carrying. They ransacked the bus within a space of at most five minutes and they disappeared in a huff, leaving behind the hapless passengers. None had the capacity, nor the courage to protest, after all they knew protesting would mean sure death by hacking. Some of the women passengers were crying as they had been robbed of their gold jewellery, they were carrying in person. The helper and the conductor along with the driver then quickly removed the log and they started all over again.

As the bus trudged along the road, the darkness spilt fear and anguish on the passengers. They had not even covered some two kilometres when they were again stopped by a group of men, wearing the fatigues they had met earlier. Then again, they boarded the bus and much to the astonishment of the puzzled passengers started handing the looted items back to the passengers.

Mr. Ramprakash was handed over the gold wedding ring, and the cash. So were the other passengers who got back their valuables.

As they were leaving, Ramprakash couldn't help but blurt out, "Why are you returning these?"

Spat came the reply, "I don't want to pay five thousand rupees from my own pocket?"

Puzzled, he enquired again, "To whom and why?"

One of them threatened and replied, "None of your business! Anyone who reports this to the police would not be spared, do you understand what I mean?"

Then the dacoits started to disappear into the darkness from where they had appeared.

Mr. Ramprakash, adamantly interjected, "You didn't reply to my question?"

The lone dacoit who was about to alight from the bus after the others, nastily replied, "Bloody hell, once a dacoity is reported, the police demands one lakh and fifty thousand rupees from us as bribes. We got only one lakh forty five thousand rupees from this dacoity. Who would pay the extra five thousand you or your granddad?"

Before Mr. Ramprakash could answer, the dacoit jumped out and disappeared in the cover of darkness. Mr. Ramprakash realized he had survived to tell the story of how "Corruption saved the day!"

****

THE UNINVITED GUIDE!

One fine day, Nilratan Samaddar called Romen Ganguly, his employee to his cabin.

He said to Romen, "Well, there is something I need to tell you urgently."

Pausing a while, he continued, "Well, Romen you know that I hail from the Rakhain village of Keranipara near Kuakata beach in Patuakhali district of Bangladesh. There is a hundred year old temple in Keranipara of Goddess Maa Kali of our village, famously known as Seema Mandir. The deity is made of a metal that consists of eight different metals. Every year, during the time of Kali puja, I visit my ancestral home, with my family. Unfortunately, this year my son, has broken his arm. I need to stay at home, to look after him. However, I need someone to go and give some money to the organizers of the Kali festival. I can always transfer the money online, but I would be grateful if you can go there yourself on my behalf!"

Romen asked, "But I have never travelled outside West Bengal, India. Let alone travel to Bangladesh. Moreover, I do not have a passport! How do you expect me to travel to Keranipara in Bangladesh!"

"I will arrange for your passport and other essential formalities. But will you go?"

"I can always go! But, is there any other option left!" he said before giving a mischievous smile.

Nilratan smiled and replied, "Well, I am relieved now! I can arrange for you to go to Dhaka by flight and then you can go to the Rakhain village Keranipara. The road distance from Dhaka to Patuakhali is 319 km. You can take a bus from Sayedabad or Gabtoli bus terminus of Dhaka to reach Patuakhali. There are two routes by bus to arrive at Patuakhali district. One goes from Dhaka via Mawa and Barisal to Patuakhali and another one drives from Dhaka via Aricha through Barisal to Patuakhali. Kuakata in the located in Patuakhali district of Bangladesh and only a few miles away to the south from Khepupara. The Rakhain Village Keranipara is located five kilometers to the east of Kuakata beach!"

The next few days were hectic for both Romen and Nilratan. Nilratan saw to it that Romen's passport was arranged and then he transferred the money to Romen's bank account for the transportation, hotel arrangements and other miscellaneous expenses. Romen was excited and had informed his family and friends about this. His friend Saikat even presented him with two packets of cigarette, saying, "Well these may become handy in Bangladesh!"

It was the two days before the "Bhoot Chaturdashi," which normally occurs on the 14th day of Krishna Paksha (waning phase of moon) on the night before Kali Puja/Diwali festival that Romen landed at Dhaka, airport. He left for his hotel by taxi. He did some sightseeing in Dhaka the next day. Then on 'Bhoot Chaturdashi' left for Patuakhali by a hired car which Nilratan had arranged.

Romen was asking the driver, Ali Asghar, about the lifestyle of people in Bangladesh.

He and Ali went on to exchange views about the two countries of Bangladesh and India.

Romen said, "I am visiting Bangladesh for the first time. I will visit the Seema Mandir, at the Rakhain village Keranipara, near Kuakata at Patuakhali."

Ali said, "It is a nice place the Rakhain population is very friendly there."

"You mean just like me?" commented Romen.

Ali laughed.

Romen continued, "Tomorrow is Kali puja, it is a very big festival in West Bengal. Well, today is 'Bhoot Chaturdoshi' you know! In West Bengal, on this night, Bengalis light fourteen earthen-lamps (choddo prodip) at their homes to appease the spirits of their past fourteen generations of ancestors. It is believed that today, the night before Kali Puja, the spirits of these ancestors descend upon earth, and these lamps help them find their loving homes. Another popular belief is that Chamunda (a fearsome aspect of Kali) along with 14 other ghostly forms ward off the evil spirits from the house as 14 earthen-lamps are lit at different entrances and dark corners of the house. Also, it is customary to consume a dish of 14 different types of spinach or cress (choddo shaak). They may include amaranth, radish green, red amaranth, water spinach, spinach, mustards green, fenugreek greens, young jute greens, turnip greens, chickpea greens, bottle gourd greens, Ceylon spinach, pumpkin green, taro greens, centella, and basella/Malabar Spinach, to name a few of them during Bhoot Chaturdashi. These are consumed so that evil spirits cannot possess the body. Scientifically, other than traditional and the ritualistic part these greens have much medicinal properties which help to build our immune system. By the way, do you believe in ghosts in Bangladesh? "

Ali replied, "We in this part of Bangladesh, believe in ghosts! There are lot of haunted places in Dhaka and here also!"

It was then that the engine of the car had developed a snag and it coughed to a halt.

Romen asked Ali, "Where are we?"

"We have just crossed the Musillipara village of Kuakata," came the reply.

It was six in the evening.

Ali hurriedly tried fixing the car. Romen got down from the car and tried to relax himself by stretching his arms and legs. Romen found that he had exhausted his packet of cigarettes. So he asked Ali, if he could walk down the road to find some.

Ali replied, "If you, go straight down the road, walk around five to six minutes you will find a shop!"

Romen was walking down the road, on both sides there were trees lined up, and after going around for two three minutes, he found he had one packet of cigarettes left in his shirt pocket. He quickly lit one of the cigarettes and walked on. He felt his mood lighten up a bit while smoking the cigarette.

On one side of the road there were marshes.

Strangely, Romen found that there was a strange light looking like a flying, glowing orb of fire in the marshes.

There was no one around, so he left the road and walked towards the marshes. It appeared and then it disappeared. He was drawn towards it. He was at the edge of the water, when suddenly, a voice startled him from behind. He turned around to find a pot-bellied Brahmin, who was bare chested wearing a dhoti and a sacred thread (poitay/yajnopavita or janeu).

Romen asked, "Did you see that?"

The Brahmin smiled and replied, "You mean the strange hovering marsh-lights?"

"Yes."

"Some say they are the Aleya or 'will-o the wisp' or the ghost-lights representing the ghosts of fisherman who died fishing."

Romen laughed at this and said, "If they are the Aleya or 'will-o the wisp' then I must be a 'Brahmodaittyo' (ghost of the Brahmin)."

The Brahmin smiled and replied, "What do you know about Brahmodaittyos, young man?"

Romen smiled and said, "Well, they are very kind and helpful to human beings like you and me and benevolent as well."

"Where are you from? You don't appear from this place?"

"Well, since you asked, I am from Kolkata, West Bengal, India."

"Where are you heading?"

Romen mischievously smiled and replied, "Where the Aleya would lead a Brahmodaittyo?"

"You have a good sense of humour. Speaking of ghosts, the

Rakhaine people of Musullipara village at Kuakata believe that there are ghosts. It was in the late 1980s that a father and son duo from Musullipara village at Kuakata went into the deep forest of Gangamati by the Bay of Bengal to collect fuel wood. Just like other local fishermen do! At some point of time both felt thirsty. As is the common practice, they both started to dig the sandy surface with their hands in search of water. As they removed the sand over a small area, they sensed that they hit something precious. They found a wooden structure embossed with golden decorative sheets. The duo, with their wood cutting machete dismantled the golden bits and then started to dig further for more. The more they dug, more of the metals emerged from what it looked like a very large wooden boat buried under the sand filled with gold. They were exhausted by the end of the day. As the sun was about to set, both of them decided to call it a day and left the place promising to return early next morning. The father and son never again saw the light of day. During the night both died under mysterious circumstances, prompting widespread gossip among people of the Kuakata. Soon people learnt about the buried boat in the forest laden with gold. The unexplained deaths of the father and son duo, who had collected "gold" from the mysterious boat, triggered another rumor suggesting that the boat was cursed and haunted. Till today many people in Kuakata believe that anyone trying to explore the gold-laden boat would face the same fate of the father and son."

"Good story! But they didn't explain the mysterious lights over the marshes!"

"Well some say the father son duo entices men into the swamps in search of the gold-laden boat, which is why the simmering lights of the last rays of the sun actually reflect the gold-laden boat. Then the father-son duo kills off the unsuspecting fellow!"

"But then who are you?" asked Romen.

"Well, should I say the benevolent Brahmodaittyo who is trying to lead you from harm's way from the innocuous ghosts of the father son duo!"

Romen started laughing aloud, this time.

Romen joked, "Then I would call you Mr. Brahmodaittyo!"

The Brahmin smiled and replied, "Well, as you wish!"

"By the way, how far is the beach from here?"

"Not far, come I will show you around, things that you will remember throughout your life!" said the Brahmin.

Romen followed the Brahmin as they briskly walked from dyke of the marshland. They went through a bamboo garden. Suddenly, a man came and asked, "Thakurmoshai (priest), where are you off to?" referring to the Brahmin.

The Brahmin replied, "Don't pester me, will you, Mesho (uncle)!"

The manner in which the Brahmin said, "Mesho," Romen had

heard "Besho."

Then the man again interjected, "Who is this?"

The Brahmin replied, "A friend of ours who thinks Brahmodaittyos are benevolent!"

The man laughed and replied, "He has a nice sense of humour. Go in peace."

Romen didn't speak up but later when they had crossed the bamboo garden.

Romen joked, "Alright, Mr. Brahmodaittyo, was the gentleman we just saw, your Mesho (uncle) or "Besho?""

Besho Bhoot (ghosts of the bamboo garden) were common in these parts of Bangladesh, as Romen had heard.

The Brahmin smiled and replied, "You can call him what you want."

By then they had come to a clearing. There was a big field, sparsely dotted with banayan and shiyora trees.

"I live there," said the Brahmin and then pointed towards a certain direction where a certain banyan tree stood. As the last remnants of the fading sunlight were disappearing, Romen could make some lights beyond the banyan tree. He joked as usual, "You call yourself a Brahmodaittyo, pointing to lights beyond the banyan tree. That's not fair. You should live atop the banyan tree!"

Now the Brahmin laughed out aloud.

"Be our guest tonight. Gentleman from Kolkata."

"I have come far, I don't think I can go any further. I had come for some cigarettes, but I found I had a packet of them left in my shirt pocket. I think I have to return to the main road because, Ali, my driver is waiting for me."

"I will give you a smoke the hookah. We have the finest tobacco here!" insisted the Brahmin.

So Romen relented although almost unwillingly.

By then the shadows of the trees were getting lengthier and evolving into shadows that seemed to dance to the faint tune of some mesmerizing music, that was floating in from beyond the field. He found only bats hovering in the horizon. Romen could feel a strange attraction that was pulling him towards the music. It reminded him of the lullabies he had heard from his grandmother when he was a kid!

"Come with me, please!" insisted the Brahmin.

Then they crossed over the field and passed through a mango orchard. They came along a pond with ghats.

There Romen found a mesmerizing beautiful woman taking a bath. She was waist deep in water.

She turned and looked at Romen, then she said, "Who is our guest tonight, Thakurmoshai?"

Romen proactively replied, "I am Romen, from Kolkata."

She twitched her eyebrows and gave such a disarming look at Romen, his senses got numb. Romen felt the woman was winking at him, He was thinking, "What a lecherous woman she is." The woman had long curls of thick wet hair that reached down her waist and her white peach skin were glowing in the night. The white saree was wet and drops of water was oozing out of her white petticoat. Her perfect smile was mesmerizing and unnerving Romen. She splashed some water and took a dip in the greenish coloured water.

Then she said to Romen, "Won't you like to take a dip with me?"

The Brahmin interjected, "Go away, Buri. Leave him alone, will you!"

Suddenly Romen came out of his trance and followed the Brahmin.

"Who was she?" enquired Romen.

"She is Buri. She was jilted by her lovers and was abused by an older husband, who passed away. Her unsatisfied desires attracts young men like you. Beware of such women, Romen! She is a wicked bitch. She is waiting for her lovers to come back. She is…, I guess a living dead who is in search of that eternal love!"

By then the faint sound of the music was getting louder. By then they were standing in front of the big old zamindar haveli. The

Corinthian pillars adored the mansion. The entire courtyard was decorated with jasmine flowers. The smell was so intoxicating! There were lamps that lit the lobby of the haveli. The flames of the lamps were flickering and dancing to the tune of the music, so were the shadows! It was indeed a strange sight! There they were greeted by an old rickety man, who the Brahmin introduced as, "Kana." Then the Brahmin scolded the old man and said, "You, bugger sleeping your head off not to entertain our guest from Kolkata. Are the arrangement of the festivities made for the day?"

Kana replied, "Sorry, an afternoon nap that extended a bit longer!" Then he smiled with his remaining two teeth jutting out of a mouth that smelled of tari (local alcoholic drink) and paan (betel leaf)!"

Romen was thirsty. So he asked, "Can I get to drink some water?"

"Will some drinks do?" asked Kana.

"It's better if you could like me some water."

Then Kana caught hold of Romen's hand and took him to one of the rooms. There was a big earthen pot and he took some water in a brass glass and handed it to Romen. Romen who was thirsty gulped in the liquid only to realize that the water was stale and it was horrid to drink. So he quickly spit it out. Kana stuck his tongue out of his mouth and then sticking it in replied, "Sorry Sir, the water is not fresh. I think it is better for you if I give you a couple of our drinks."

Romen a little annoyed by now asked, "Where is

Thakurmoshai?"

Kana said, "Well, please come with me, babu!"

Then he took Romen to the inside courtyard of the house. Romen found Thakurmoshai, along with him there were four other gentlemen. Two of them were dressed like the zamindars of yester years. Romen taken aback by this didn't say anything. He was however cajoled by the Brahmin, who said, "Let me introduce you, Romen to our Zamindar Mukunda Narayan Thakur and his son Pabitra Narayan Thakur."

Both of them were dressed in immaculate white kurta pyjamas and they had golden bracelets around their wrists and jasmine garlands in their hand. They were smoking a two water hookahs. The smell of tobacco and incense were invading the air. They were lying inclined on the satin covered bed with bolsters.

They folded their hands to say Namaste to their guest and then Romen was given a flatbed covered with soft white linen cloth, and a petrolish to lie down and listen to the music. Romen now noticed that they were two more footmen who were standing behind the zamindars, none other than the musicians. They were attired in kurta and dhoti and had a turban on their head. The footmen were strong and had huge mustaches. Each had a strong stick in their hand. Of the other two gentleman, both were musicians. One of them was playing the esraj and the other was playing the tabla. Suddenly the older gentleman who was playing the esraj, started playing the raag

Jhinjyoti. Then the sound of the esraj and the tabla reverberated and it echoed around the entire haveli.

Romen was served with a glass of drinks by Kana.

Romen thirsty as he was, drank it all. The Thakurmoshai didn't forget to pass one of the hookahs for Romen to smoke tobacco. The fresh tobacco instilled some energy in Romen.

"Usher in Churni will you!" ordered Pabitra Narayan Thakur.

Then the dance began as a woman of plus size, started erotically gyrating to the music played by the two musicians. The dance seemed to go on forever, as Romen lost count of time. When the dance finished, Pabitra asked Romen, "Want some more of this?"

Romen amused by this hospitality had replied in the affirmative.

"Call in Chini then!"

Again, the mesmerizing music started and in came another young ravishing maiden who started dancing elegantly and enticingly to satisfy Romen's eyes! By then, Romen had drank too much. When she finished, she sat beside Romen and started caressing Romen's feet with her nimble cold hands. Other dancers had taken over. Her touch was arousing Romen. Slowly it started to drive him wild. But still he didn't say anything. Suddenly, as the proximity between the two started diminishing, Thakurmoshai interjected. He said to Chini, "Leave him alone will you! He is as innocent as a flower! Even Buri couldn't mesmerize him!"

To this comment, Chini started laughing hysterically and then she replied, "So am I!" The effect of the drinks had started, Romen found that his senses were again becoming numb. The music, drinks, the smell of tobacco and his tiredness all were adding up. He tried to stay awake, but slowly he started to succumb to the enemy called sleep. Suddenly his mobile phone started ringing. He realized that he had to go back to his car where Asghar was waiting. He wanted to jump up, but his senses and his body had given way to the drinks and the tiredness. However, he fell asleep without picking up his phone.

Meanwhile, by the time Asghar the driver had finished, he tried to calling up Romen. Romen's phone was out of reach for some time and then when it rang, no one was picking it up. It was late at night by then so Asghar thought he would inform Nilratan about this. So he called Nilratan and relayed what had transpired. By then Nilratan was worried sick. Nilratan called up Romen, his phone went on ringing but no one picked it up. Nilratan called up Mr. Abdul Rahman and asked if he could help. Mr. Rahman an old friend of Nilratan asked Nilratan to wait until the morning and then go in search for Romen.

It was not until nine in the morning that Romen woke up. He felt dizzy. He found himself on a floor of a courtyard of a dilapidated haveli. He tried to recall, but his senses were numb. He realized that his phone was ringing incessantly. He reached for his phone and when he answered it, he found an unknown voice enquiring about his whereabouts.

He asked, "Who is this speaking?"

"I am Abdul Rahman, friend of Nilratan. But where are you?"

"I don't recall!" replied Romen.

He looked around and replied, "Possibly, it looks like I was sleeping on the floor of the courtyard of some dilapidated mansion or haveli I guess!"

"What?"

"You had all of us worried sick? But why were you not picking up the phone?"

"I was sleeping."

"What is the address of the place?"

"I don't recall!" replied Romen.

"Are you ok?"

"Yes!"

"Are you hurt?"

"No."

"Where are you then?"

Slowly Romen was regaining his senses and he realized that something queer and unexplainable had taken place with him yesterday. Then he remembered meeting the Brahmin, and his memory was back in a jiffy. However, the question that was baffling him was, "Where was Thakurmoshai? Where was Kana? Where were the musicians? What about the Zamindar and his son? Where were the footmen and the dancers?"

Again Abdul asked Romen, "What do you see around yourself?"

Romen replied, "Ruins and a slithering black snake!"

"Snakes?"

"Yes, a small one at other end of the courtyard!"

Then Romen said, "I don't understand, there was a Thakurmoshai who brought me here. There were some other people as well. But where is everyone? Where are the hookahs? Where is the bed with soft linen cloth, the wine glasses, everything seems to be missing!"

Romen continued agitatedly, "Well, yesterday there were flowers, the courtyard was clean, but now I find filth and dead leaves all around. The wooden windows are all broken, discoloured and hanging from the sill. The stench of dead leaves is terrible. Creepers had invaded and the place is damp and cold! It appears no one has come to this place for years! There are cobwebs all around. But why am I here?"

"Do you do drugs?"

Romen replied a little annoyed, "What sort of question is this? Do you think I am crazy? I only smoke cigarettes and have a drink or two! But I never do drugs!"

"I guess it was an obvious question, since you don't know where you are?"

"Well, I think I am a bit disoriented due to the drinks offered to me last night! But that's all. I am telling you the truth!"

"Don't you see anyone around?"

"No!"

"Can you come out of the building that you are in?"

"It is not a building; it is all in ruins!"

"Can you come out? But whatever you do don't disconnect the call!"

Romen got up and walked out of the haveli only to be blinded by the strong sunlight. He cursed.

"What happened?"

"Nothing! It is the sun, it had temporarily blinded me! I am already out, now!"

"What do you see around?"

"The ruins of a haveli that I left behind and the pond with ghats, where the lady named Buri with long hair was bathing?"

"Is she still there?"

"No!"

"Can you see anyone around?"

"No!"

"Can you retrace your path back?"

"Yes, I think I can!"

"Don't panic, just stay calm!"

"I am over the phone, just walk back will you!"

Romen started telling Abdul what had happened.Abdul Rahman's worst nightmares were coming true. He realized that Romen might have been hypnotized by a ghost and taken to some unknown location. Romen, instead of reaching his destination, went to the haunted grounds. After that Romen must have lost his senses. The only hope was that the mobile connection was still working, hence the place was not far off from the human habitable locality.

Romen slowly made his way through the mango orchard and then the field of the banyan and shiyora trees. Then he crossed the bamboo garden alone and reached the dyke of the marshes. Slowly he made his way back to the road.

All the while, Abdul was speaking to him and encouraging him to return to where he had started. Then he found a shop where he asked for a cigarette and bought a packet of thistle. The thistle was so tasty that Romen ate two packets of it. He was dead tired, and recovering from being a bit disoriented when Abdul found him waiting at the shop.

Then he took him to Keranipara. He was now in safe hands. He took him to his house and asked him to tell him whatever he had remembered. Romen had narrated everything that had transpired.

Mr. Gafur Rahman, Abdul's father whom Romen related his story, said, "You are very lucky!"

Romen had asked, "Why?"

Mr. Gafur had said, "You were possibly lured, by an Aleya. Well, in the marshes of Bangladesh, this phenomenon is common. You were possibly hypnotized and taken by a Kanabhulo! Kanabhulo is a ghost that hypnotizes a person, and takes him to some unknown haunted grounds. Possibly something very similar happened with you. There you met with a bunch of ghosts, including the benevolent Brahmodaittyo. After all, it was Bhoot chaturdoshi, remember! Chunni was possibly the short form of Shakchunni that is derived from the Sanskrit word Shankhachurni. It is the ghost of a married woman who wears traditional bangles."

Mr. Gafur ruminated for some time and then said, "Buri was possibly the ghost of sheekol buri. These are the ghosts of young women, who committed suicide by drowning due to an unhappy marriage. These type of ghosts may have also formed due to the death of women who may have been violently drowned against their own will after being impregnated with unwanted children by unscrupulous men. They would return to the earth and must then live out their designated time on earth before they are set free. Just like many of the fairies, these ghosts sometimes do take human lovers. Sheekol Buris' main purpose is to prowl and lure young men and take them into the depths of waterways where they would entangle the feet of their mortal lover with their long hair and submerge them. The hair of these ghosts are very long and always wet, and their eyes are without any iris. Unfortunately, these unions would end tragically for the men who are enticed by them. As it is the usual practice, they extract a promise from their mortal lovers and if such a promise is ever broken, the ghost would reveals herself to be the supernatural creature, often taking the life of the human in the process and then they become free. The general habitat of these ghosts are the water bodies!"

Mr. Gafur paused a while and then continued, "Chini was possibly the female version of Pischach often called Pishachini, who are usually hideous but may sometimes appear in the devious disguise of a young beautiful maiden to lure young men. The ghosts would drain the blood and virility of their mortal lovers. She dwells in places associated with death and filth that you found yourself in! There are a lot of these haunted places in Bangladesh. You should have been more careful!"

When he had finished, Abdul said, "I had heard of the infamous haunted house of Mukunda Narayan Thakur, that lies in beside the road near Mussillipara village. Folklore has it that Mukunda

Narayan was a tyrannical Zamindar, who lived in this place three hundred years ago! Some say he was cursed by the brahmin, whose daughter was raped by the Zamindar's son. Then a strange disease ravaged the surrounding places, and the entire Zamindar's family was wiped out. Later the Brahmin had also committed suicide. I have heard, that the Zamindar was however very fond of music. Some people say they have heard music coming from behind the bamboo garden, where there is the haunted haveli. But that was what I thought as petty folklore. I never believed it myself. I have never heard of anyone who was lured by these so called ghosts. The experience you say is terrific, something that you will hate to remember, yet love to tell others! I don't know how to explain this in rational terms. I think, you should enjoy the Kali puja here! Seek Kali Maa's blessing and go back home! Or forget this episode entirely! This is the only advice that I can give!"

Fortunately, Romen came out untouched by this. He had however, delivered the money for the intended Kali Puja given by Nilratan. After having spent an eventful journey in Bangladesh, Romen returned home just like a lovesick puppy! After reaching home, the next day he went to his friend Saikat's house where he and friends used to chat and asked, "Which of you assholes stuffed my cigarettes supplied by Saikat with weed! Had a tough time eluding this fact from the people in Bangladesh!"Rajat slowly smiled and put his hand up!

****

This story is all about characters that encompass our life. Say emotions like love, hate, joy, suffering, hope and other dimensions like time are individuals of this story. Hopefully, you will enjoy this story.

FOUR AND HALF PAGES FROM THE DIARY OF DEATH!

The mortals are a peculiar race. The rich and the powerful are always right. They decide what is right and what is wrong. If something is terribly wrong then the rules bend to make it right. Justice is sick. Justice remains the only cripple in our "class." Justice is blind! He doesn't want to be a part of it anymore though, they love to say, "Justice has been served!" These mortals like to be in control. Some of them think they control us and we think we control them.

Pride tricks them into thinking they have their way. In the end, victory is always ours!

The only doctor in our world is Time. After all, time heals everything. Time likes to fly. He teaches us life-long lessons. His service is priceless, precious yet his treatment is free. Time is impartial and is actually the same for the rich or the poor. Most mortals do not have the wisdom of spending time fruitfully. They tend to waste the service given by time. Time was an exceptional athlete in his heydays and it is practically impossible to catch up with time. Time is the only friend you will find beside you if want to spend a life wisely. He is always there for you, but if you waste his service he might not be there by your side in the long run! Time might ensure that you reach your true potential, achieve the goals and dreams!

Politics, even in our world of emotions is too hard to understand! Happy and Joy have grown up to be the best of friends. Mortals rarely even distinguish between the twins. Happy and Joy are not really that good. They are absent when you need them the most. They are lazy. Yet, they are so handsome and charming that everyone loves to be in their company. They seduce you into believing that they are your lifelong friends yet they don't stand by you in the darkest of hours. They don't deserve to be your friends, yet the mortals admire them the most. When I was young, Mr. Deeds our teacher told me, "Death, my son you are as good as your deeds!" Birth had overheard it too. I stand by mortals in the darkest of hours and do my work with clinical efficiency. Few mortals appreciate this. Neither do they appreciate my honesty! I sometimes leave them in the arms of suffering my good friend.

Birth and I are the only coloured pupils of our class. They took us in when they realized they couldn't do without us. The class had another apt pupil like me. He was Hate. I myself, have become the victim of hate so many times. He, like me, was a truly apt pupil of Mr. Deeds. He uses his devices so cunningly, that no one was spared. Not even Happy and Joy! They have ganged up against me with Fame. They are happy to hate! The saying goes, that Hate is the brains behind these all. Some say it is Greed. Hate and Greed are conniving bastards, they change their minds with the changing winds. To protect myself, I have to fight them all sometime or the other. I hate being tricked by Greed. Hate enjoys it the most when I fall prey to Greed. Yet, Justice does all in his power. He is fair they say! I like him and sometimes give him a helping hand. If you are a cripple, how much would you have to do to speak about your deeds proudly in this world?

I am possibly despised, by Fame ever since I followed Fate. I try to take away everything he has worked on and leave him with memory, hapless as a wretched cripple. Fate has taught me how to do it. Memory is the lost neglected soul who roams about aimlessly. You will find him if you are lost in the desert of thoughts. He is my favourite guide. Strange are the ways of this emotional world.

I adore Love. She has far too many admirers. She has that

kindness with which she touches every one's hearts. Her presence is felt sometimes or the other. Her absence is so very dominant, that some seek refuge under Hate, Suffering or me. She is the daughter of Beauty and Fame. Some say her father was Fate. I think she enjoys the company of Happy and Joy too.

Suffering is my only buddy who understands me! However, he is a pathetic fool. He hugs everyone so very often that they despise him. He leaves no room for privacy. He possesses some sort of nagging personality. He tries to please everyone and ends up pleasing none. He is one individual who never really deserts you even if you are lost in the desert of thoughts. I say, "Make him your friend." When you try to do that, he vanishes too. He is a coward who doesn't know if he can really value friendship. He sells wine to survive.

I love to roam like a loner when I can. Suffering follows me most often like a shadow. He is a very good tracker, rarely does he fail to track me down. He says, "I am there to fill you with the void for your desire to love!" I think he created the pangs of love to be with Love. However, I love to play hide-and-seek with him. It is one of my entertainments. Unlike him, I have many followers. They seek my help to accomplish what they want. Hate and Greed sometimes cajole them into doing that, and they remain mesmerized by their magic.

Fate, however, is the most manipulative of them all. He has developed into a shrewd and cunning personality. He sometimes directs me to steal love from Beauty and Fame. It is then that I realize that after all, he has emotional attachments too. I think he craves for love when he is alone.

Fate is a painter by profession. He is by far the most observant guy among us. He paints on the foreheads of men with his long brush. He is moody. Though he may not be the most dependable guy, yet he remains to be a very hard working man. Every day I have to fetch booze from the bar of Suffering. Suffering's ale makes him craving for more. He has slowly turned into an alcoholic. Sometimes he drinks too much and doesn't know what he is painting. He has stopped using only the gorgeous colours, which he once used. Now he is mixing them all.

He had painted the most beautiful pictures on the foreheads of Happy and joy. The riot of gorgeous colours makes them handsome. It was a long time ago when he met Beauty. Some said they had made love! Fame and Fate were the best of friends before Beauty came between them. She now walks alongside Fame. Everyone knows what a beautiful couple they make. Beauty doesn't stay long nor does Fame. Is it why they make a perfect couple? Well, Fate had it all and Fame stole her! They say, "Fate painted my forehead when he lost Beauty!" He used shades of black and gray to paint. Black reminds him of Beauty. Yet, when Fate and Fame meet they leave all their misgivings behind and chat like long lost friends. True diplomats always have their way.

Everyone rejoices these meetings apart from me and Suffering.

Fate would then break down on Suffering's lap and cry his heart out after that. Fate would then create the weakness for love in each painting. He has painted my weakness for Love too! Birth only comes close to Fate in terms of creativity. Birth is the creator and Fate paints the destiny for the creations. Mortals say Love is in the heart. But when I search it, I only find my empty creation of fear. Suffering told me, love flows in the caresses of the lovers. I try to steal her whenever I meet her! Is it why she runs away from me? Is it why she is so very timid? Sometimes she appears white as a lily and red as a rose! Is it a crime to take away my love?

I love to hunt. A thousand eyes stare at me. Some even pray that I hunt well in the hunting grounds. They cherish the moments when they shoot it with those long lenses. They are what the mortals call the "Photographers." They are just like Suffering my friend, they leave you with no privacy. I try to stay away from them, yet they are so many, it is hard to hide.

Some of my victims accompany me willingly. Some struggle because they are too much bound to Love. Some embrace me with open arms. Some don't even care. Sometimes I love to go in circles to try and confuse Suffering. I run in a circle until he is just ahead of me. The search is futile, as the shadow of Suffering envelops me with his huge frame. I am a weakling in the hands of Fate the creator. Yet can anyone blame him? Fate had it all, is what they say!

Fate sometimes plots with Hate and Greed. He would pit me and Suffering against Happy and Joy. We would fight with each other.

Usually, we win. We use fear and they fight us with humour. Hope is the perpetual optimist. He would act as the referee. He would encourage both the sides. He would help us to our feet if we lose balance. I have so many times defeated Happy and Joy. Yet they stand up again to fight against me with the inspiration from Hope. I don't think Love enjoys these fights much. She runs away whenever she hears there will be a fight. Don't we all fight for love?

I feel all of us are running in circles. These circles would intersect and at some point, we meet with each other. Briefly, though it may seem, these transitions are all but natural but the wide-eyed mortals can rarely distinguish them. I sometimes feel envious of the mortals. They are bound to us. They can still prolong these but we are bound to go around in circles. Who is the most fortunate? For once I need to feel what it is to be alive, for once I need to see what it is to carry Love in my heart and for once I need to be with Love. I will search for her till eternity. Hope always says so! He is a magician who sells dreams. Is that why we all like him so very much? Joy is actually the father of Hope! When everyone deserted, Joy would give hope! Would you like to buy dreams?

✲✲✲✲✲✲✲✲✲✲✲✲✲✲✲✲✲✲✲✲✲✲✲✲✲✲✲✲✲✲✲✲✲

ABOUT THE AUTHOR:

Shamik Dhar is a short story writer. Academically having received his education from India, U.S and U.K, he is currently employed as a QA professional in a research organization. Although he have been professionally trained as a software professional, his passion is writing short stories. It has been twenty years since he wrote his first short story. He has been influenced by famous authors like Chekov, O'Henry, Maupassant, Ruskin Bond, Mahasweta Devi and Rabindranath Tagore.

Contact Details:

Email: sdhar78@gmail.com